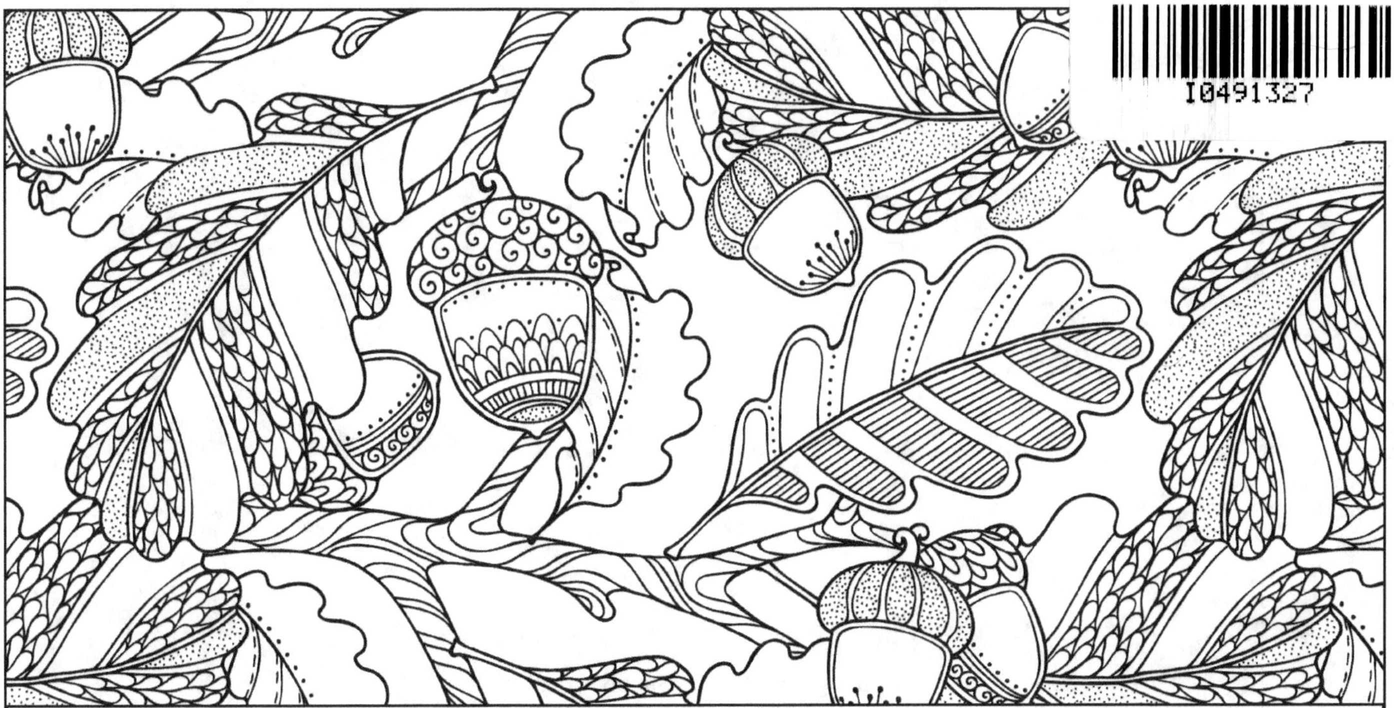

simply creative

AUTUMN
coloring book for adults

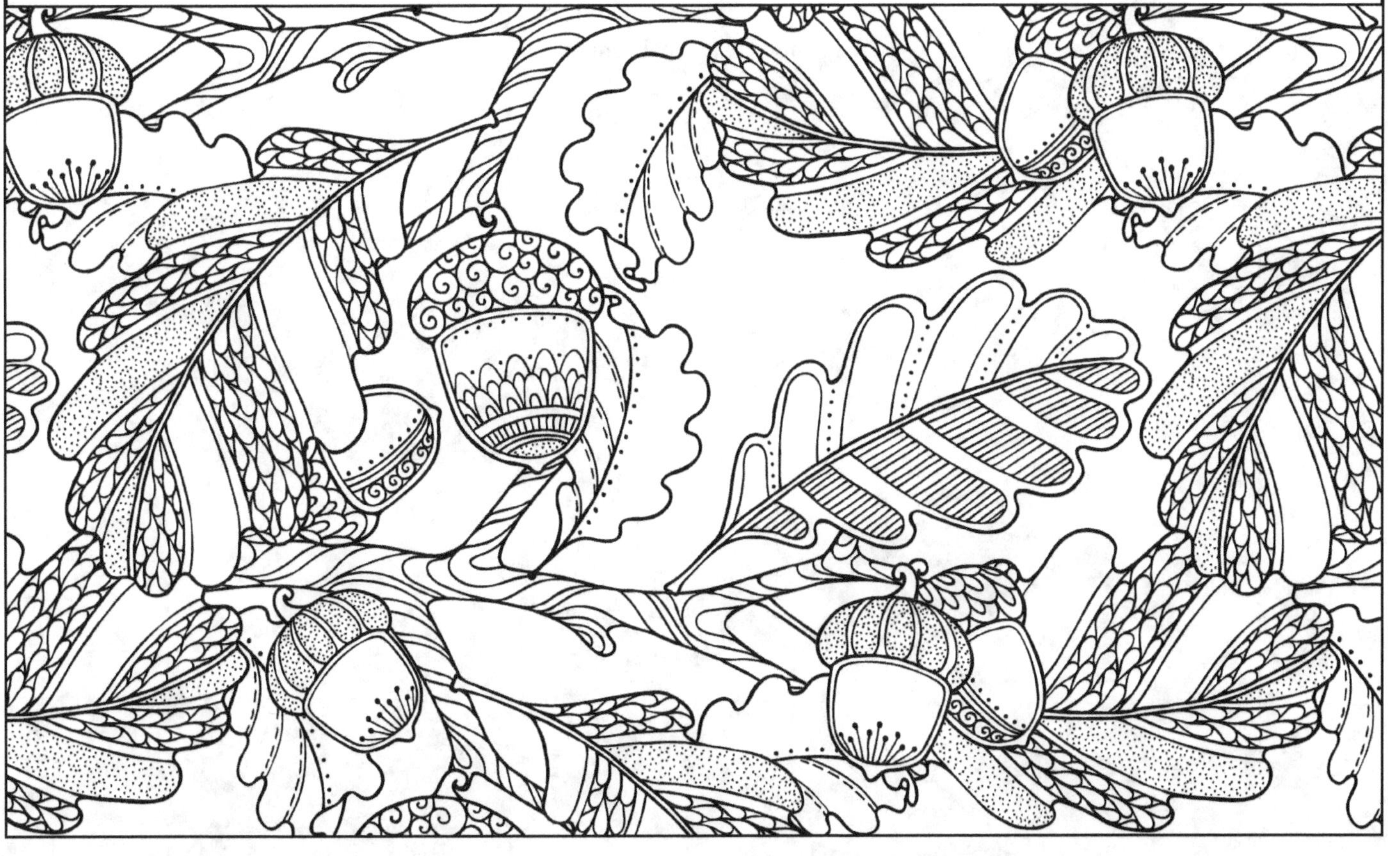

 This book belongs to:

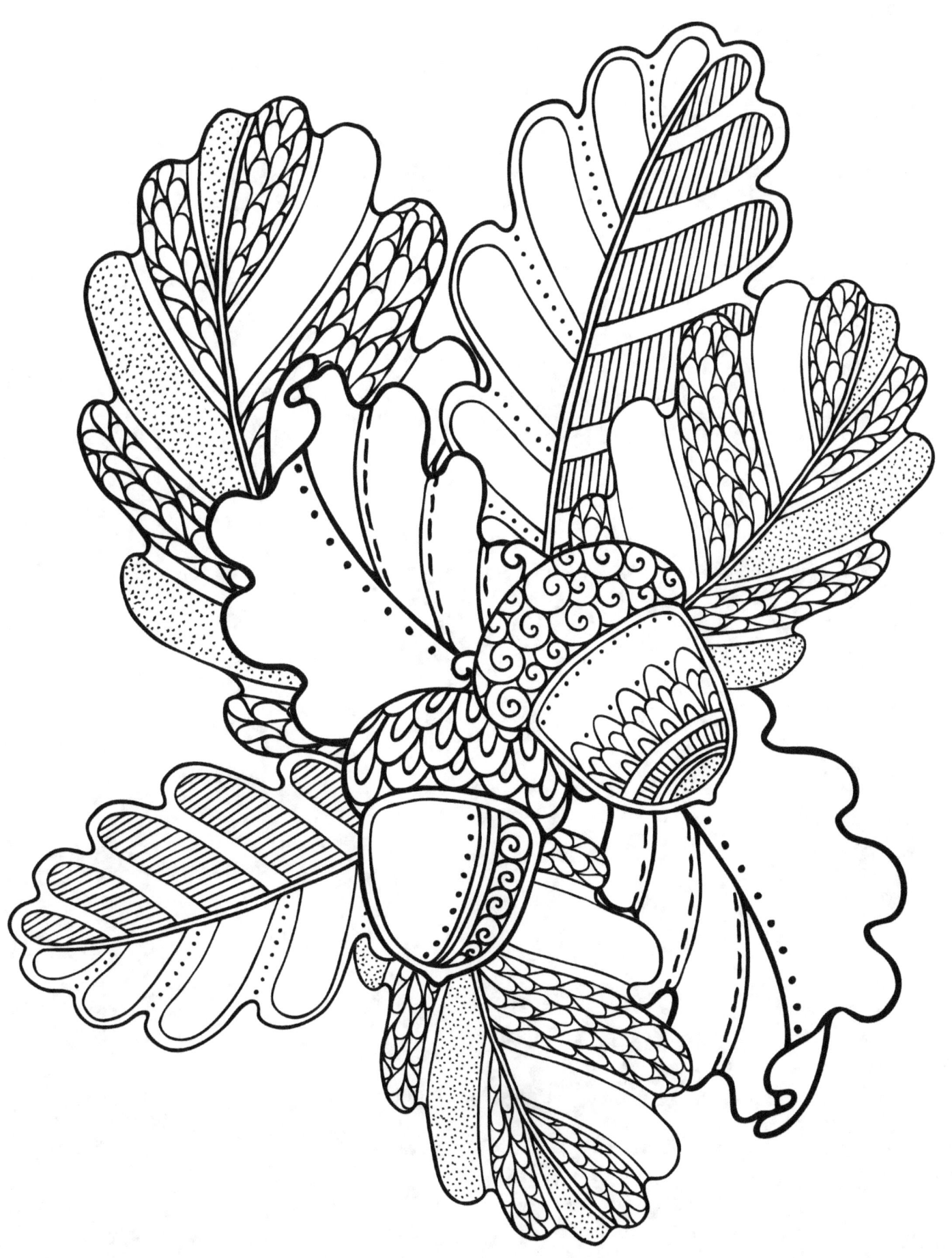

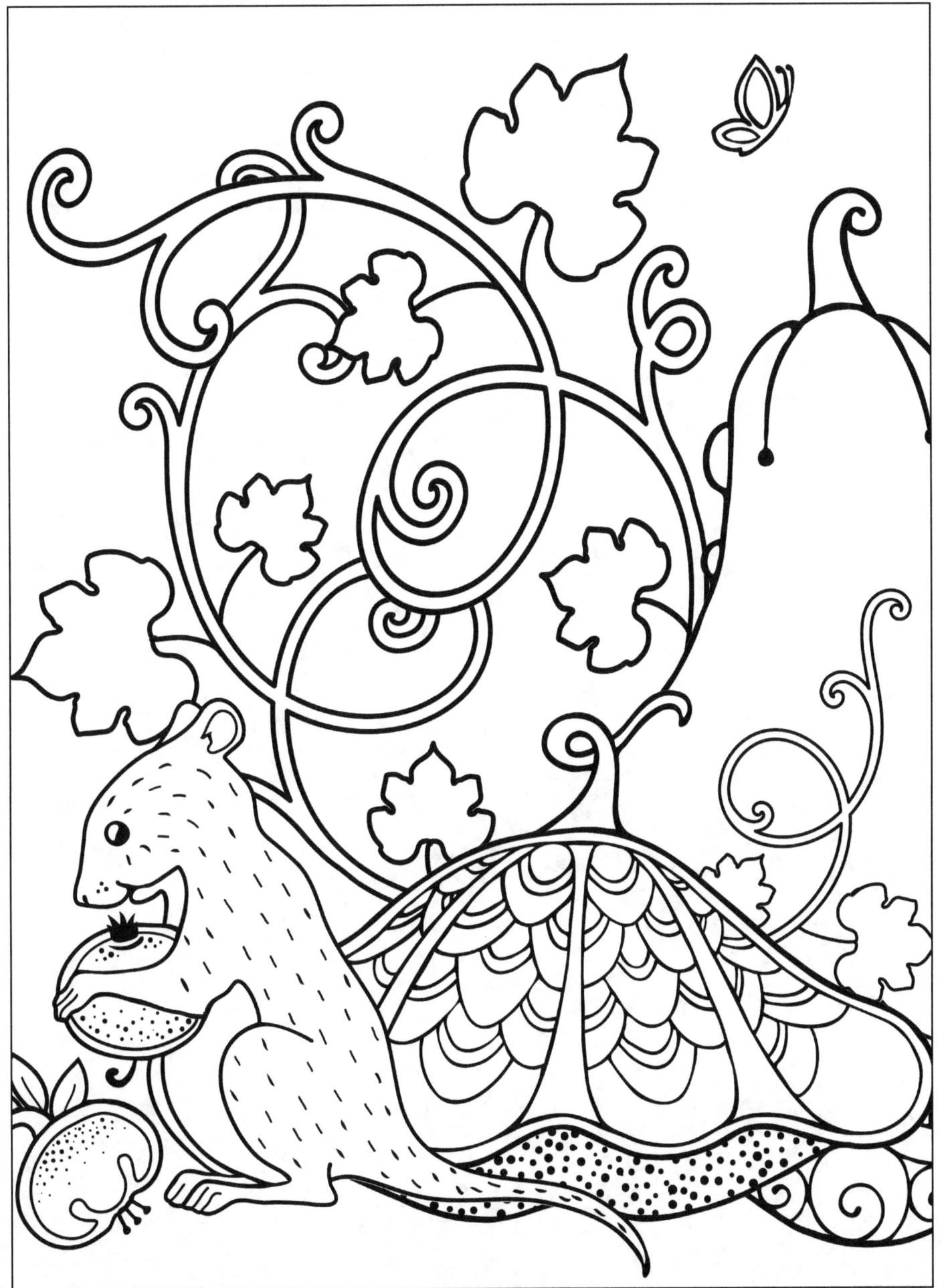

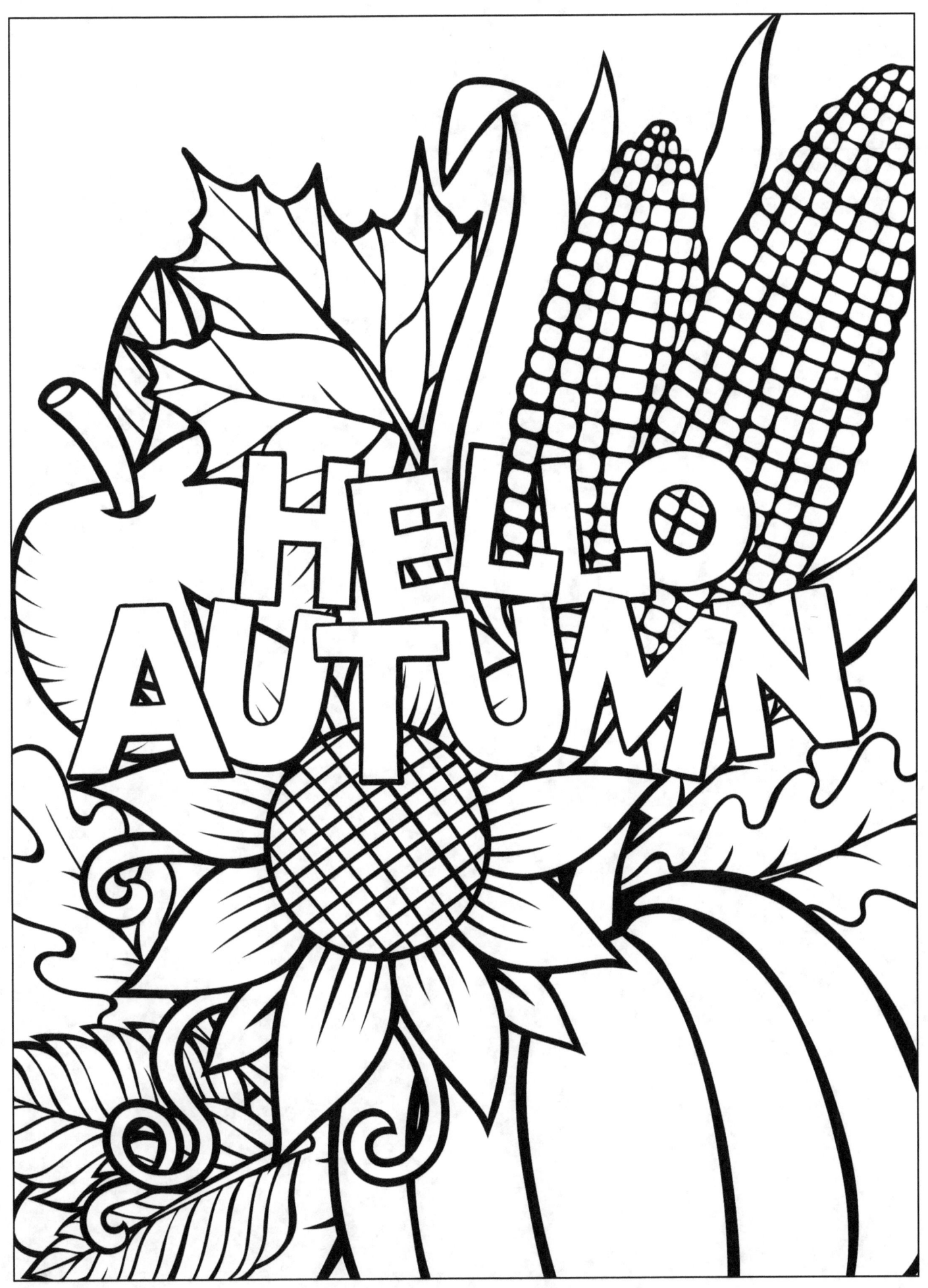

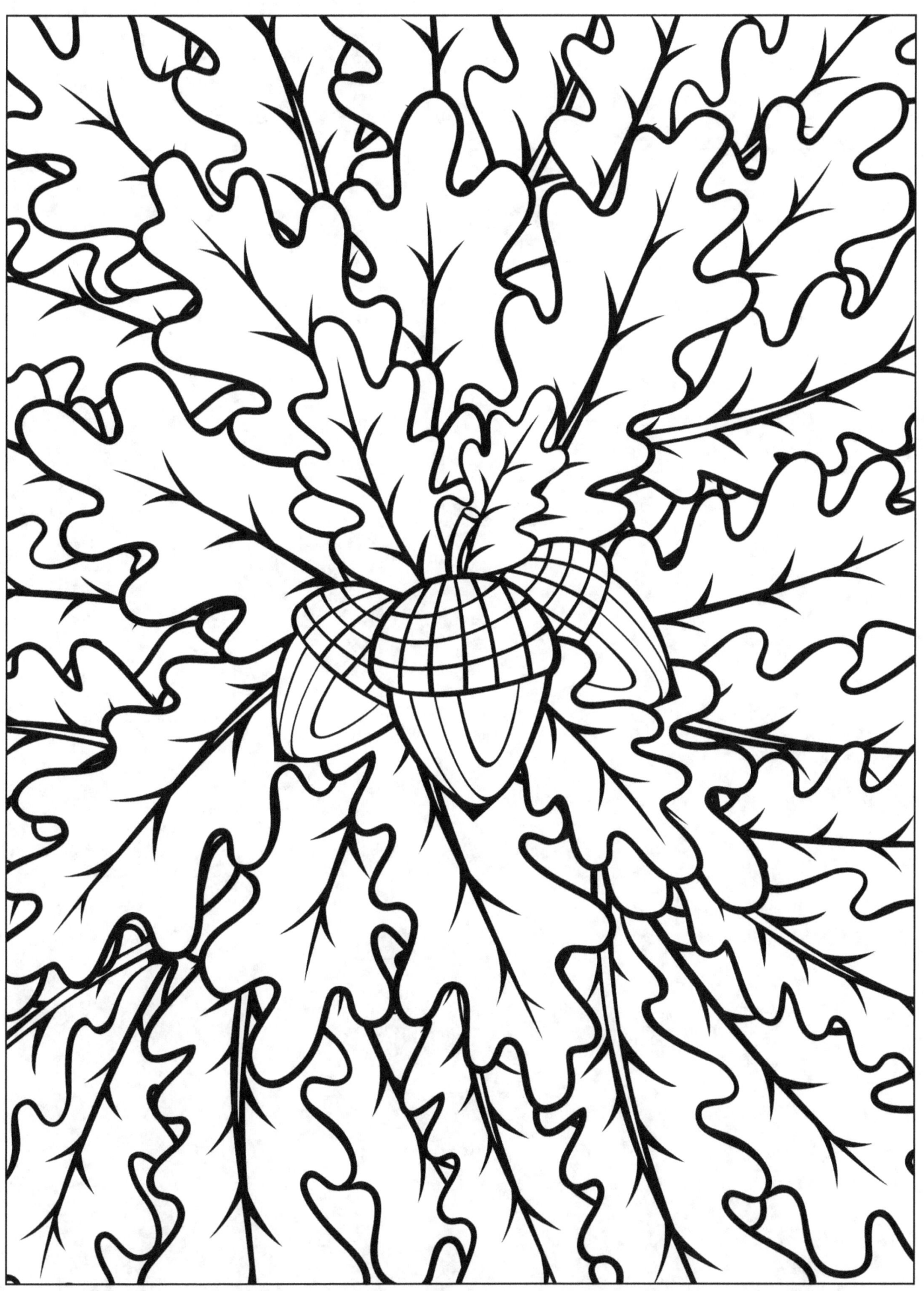

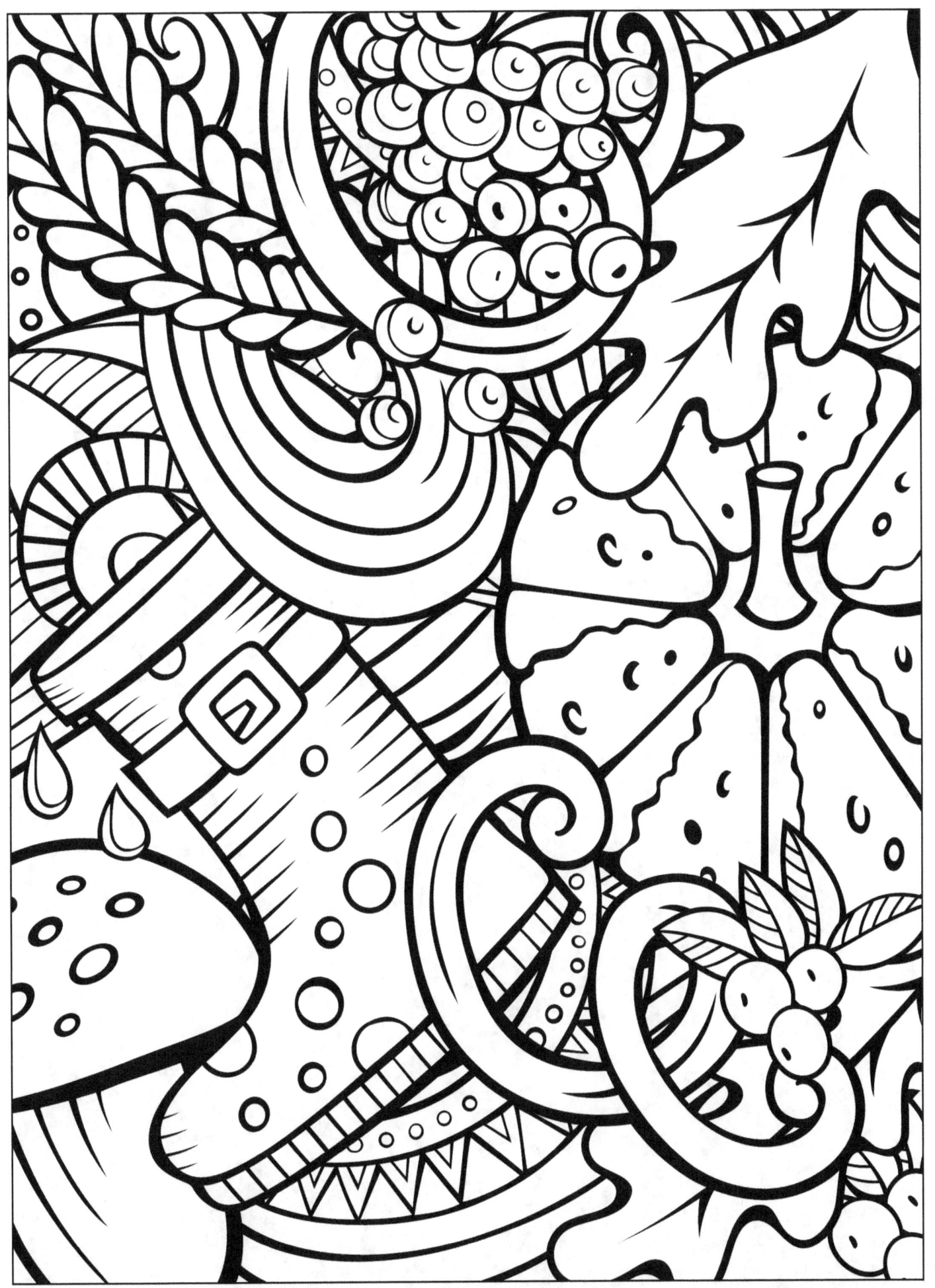

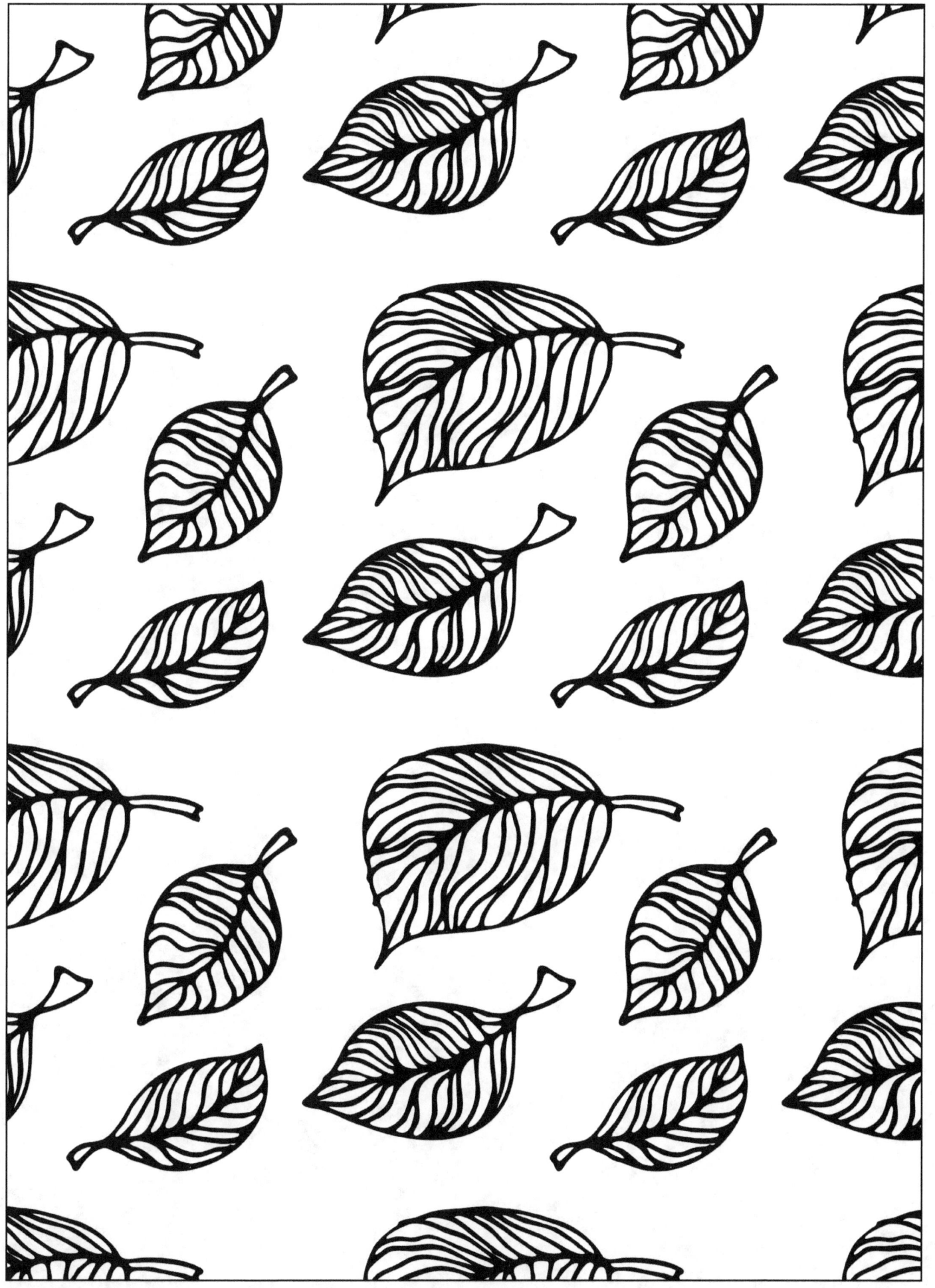

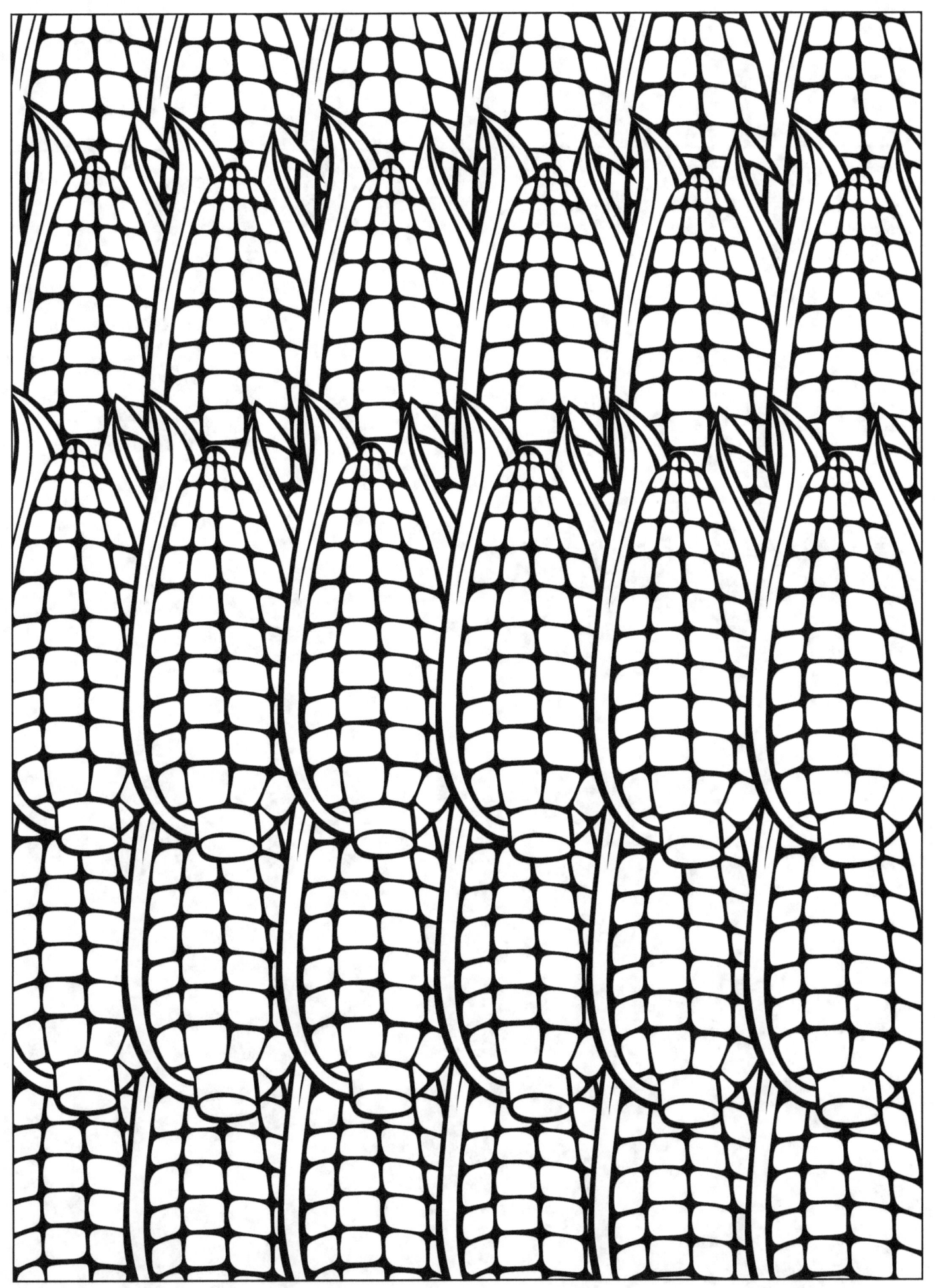

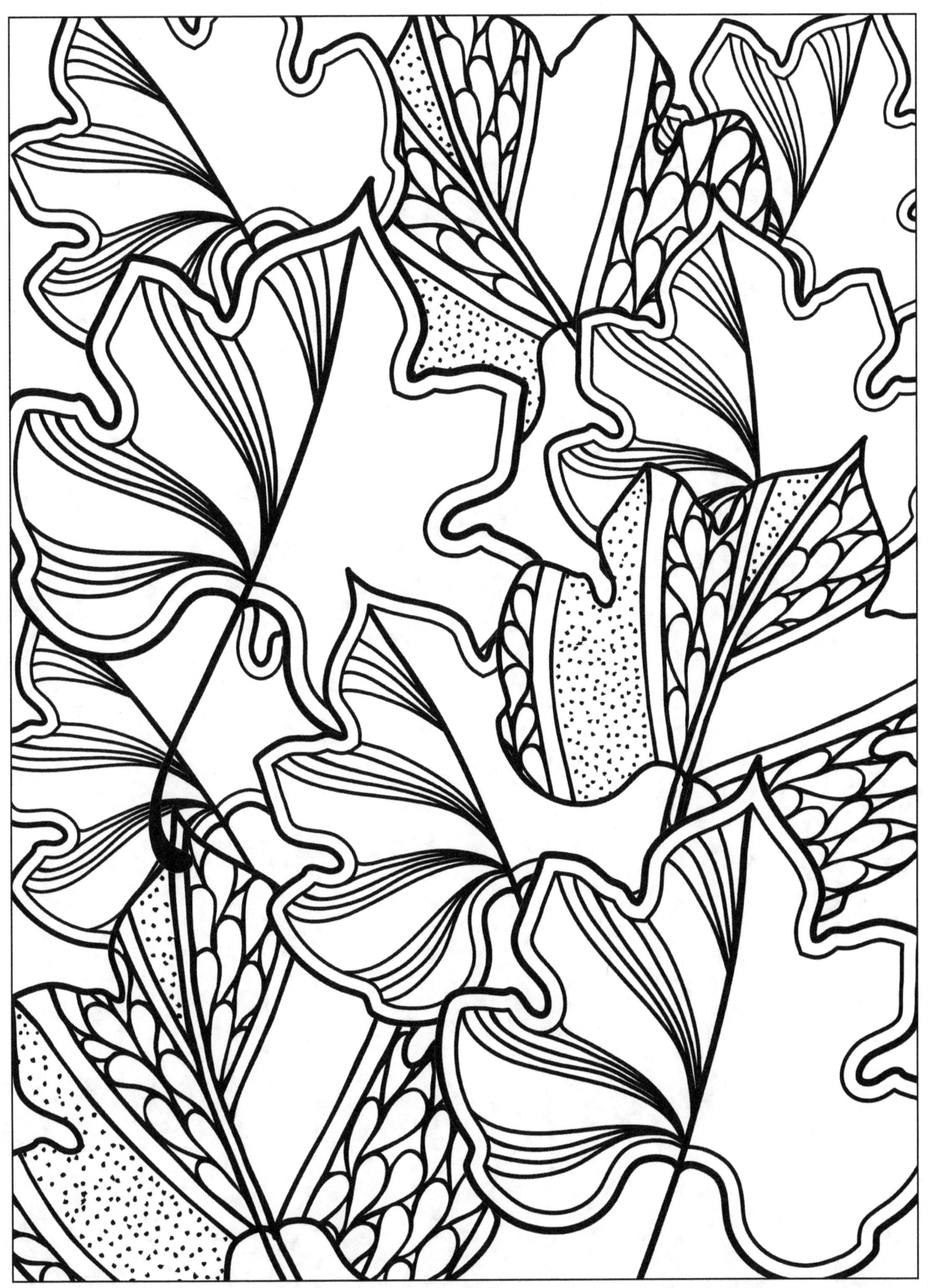

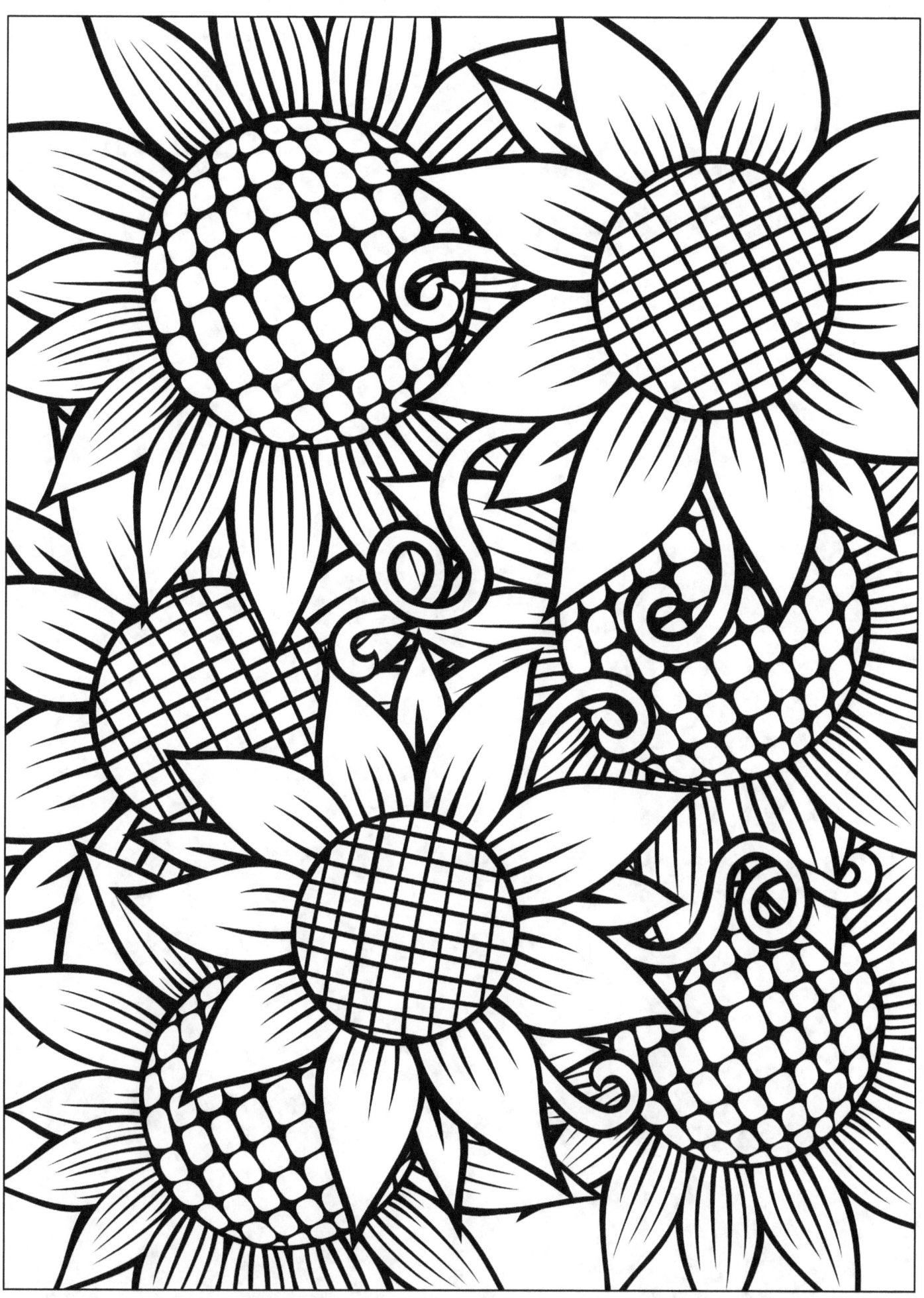

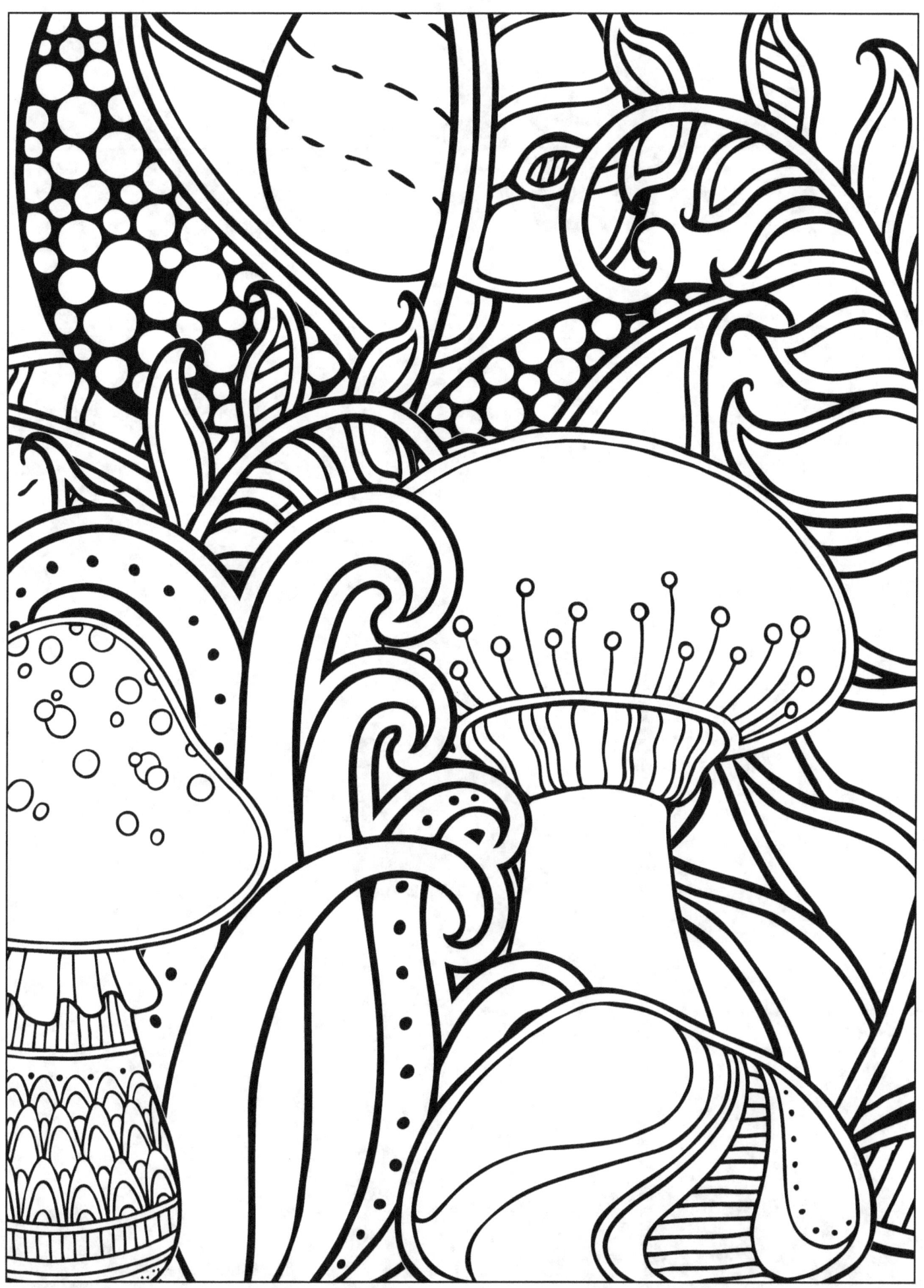

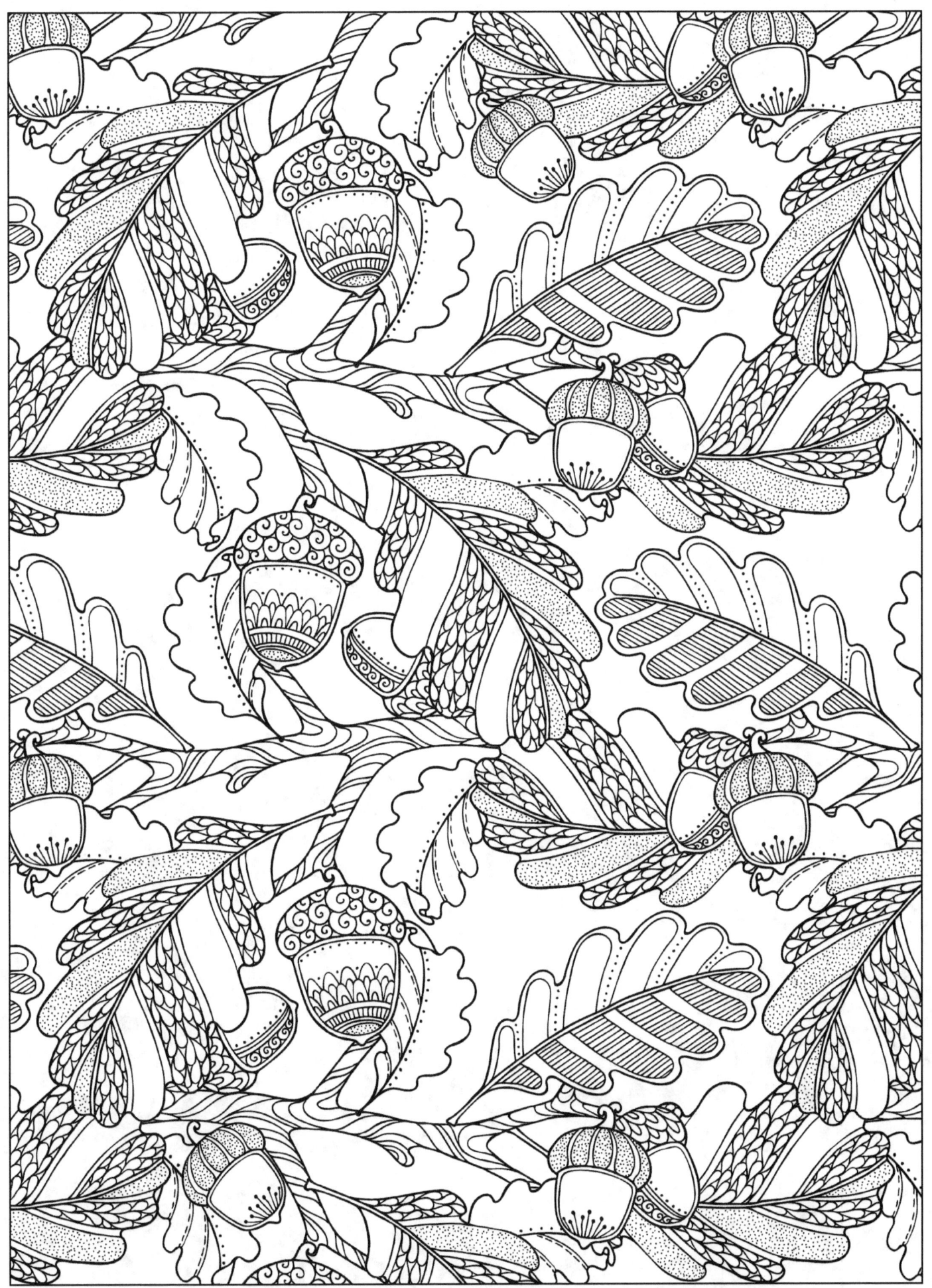

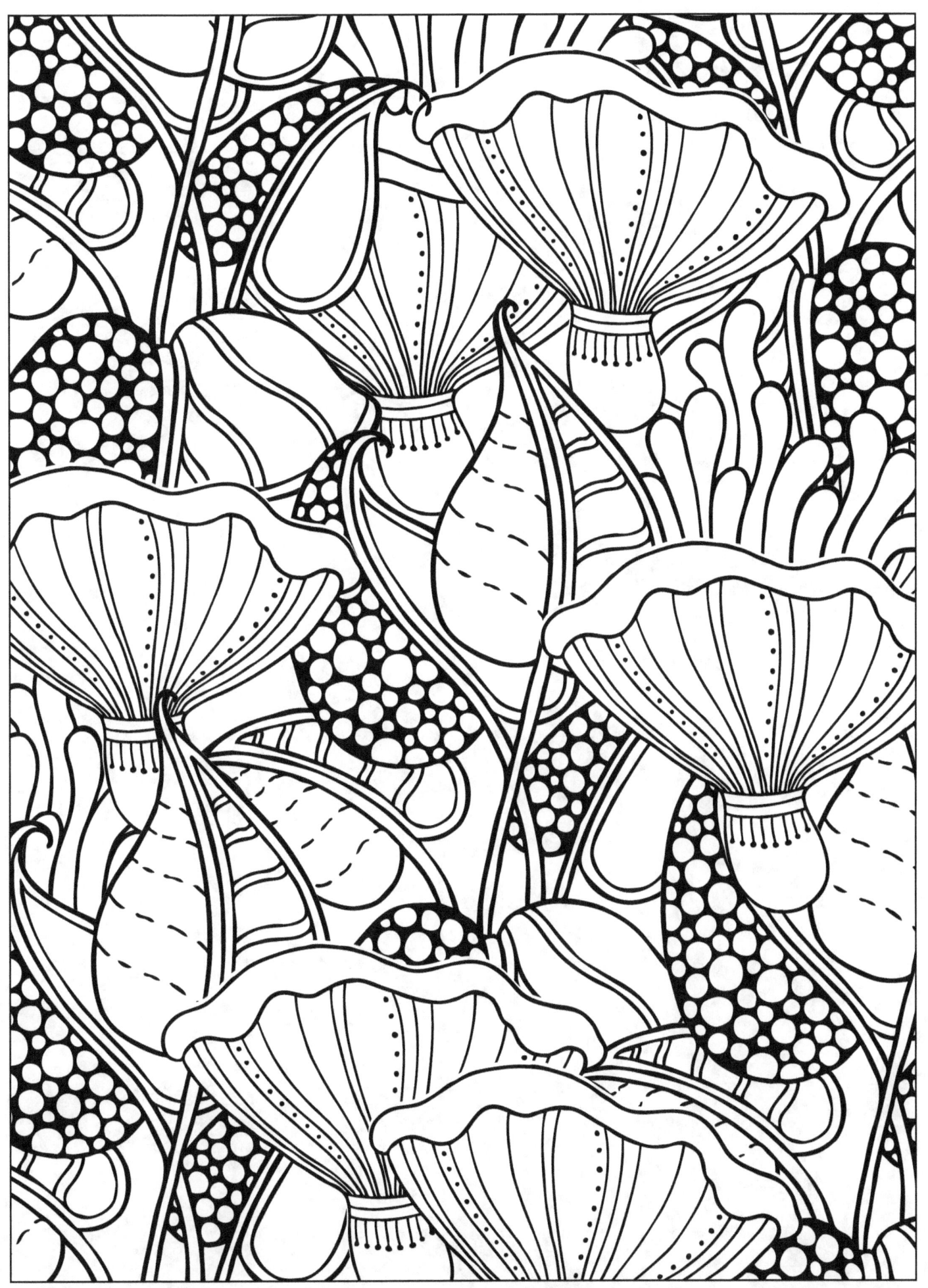

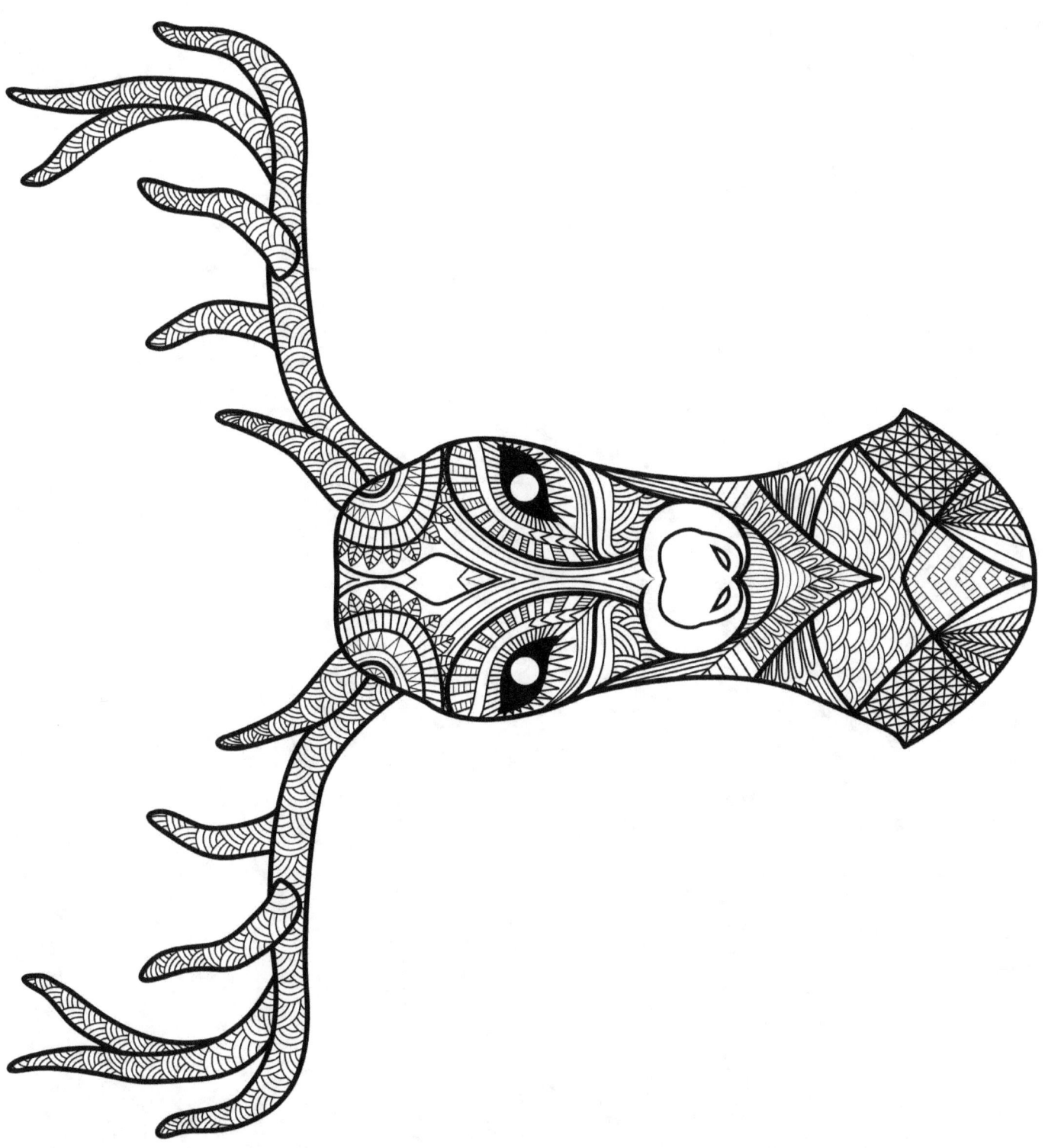

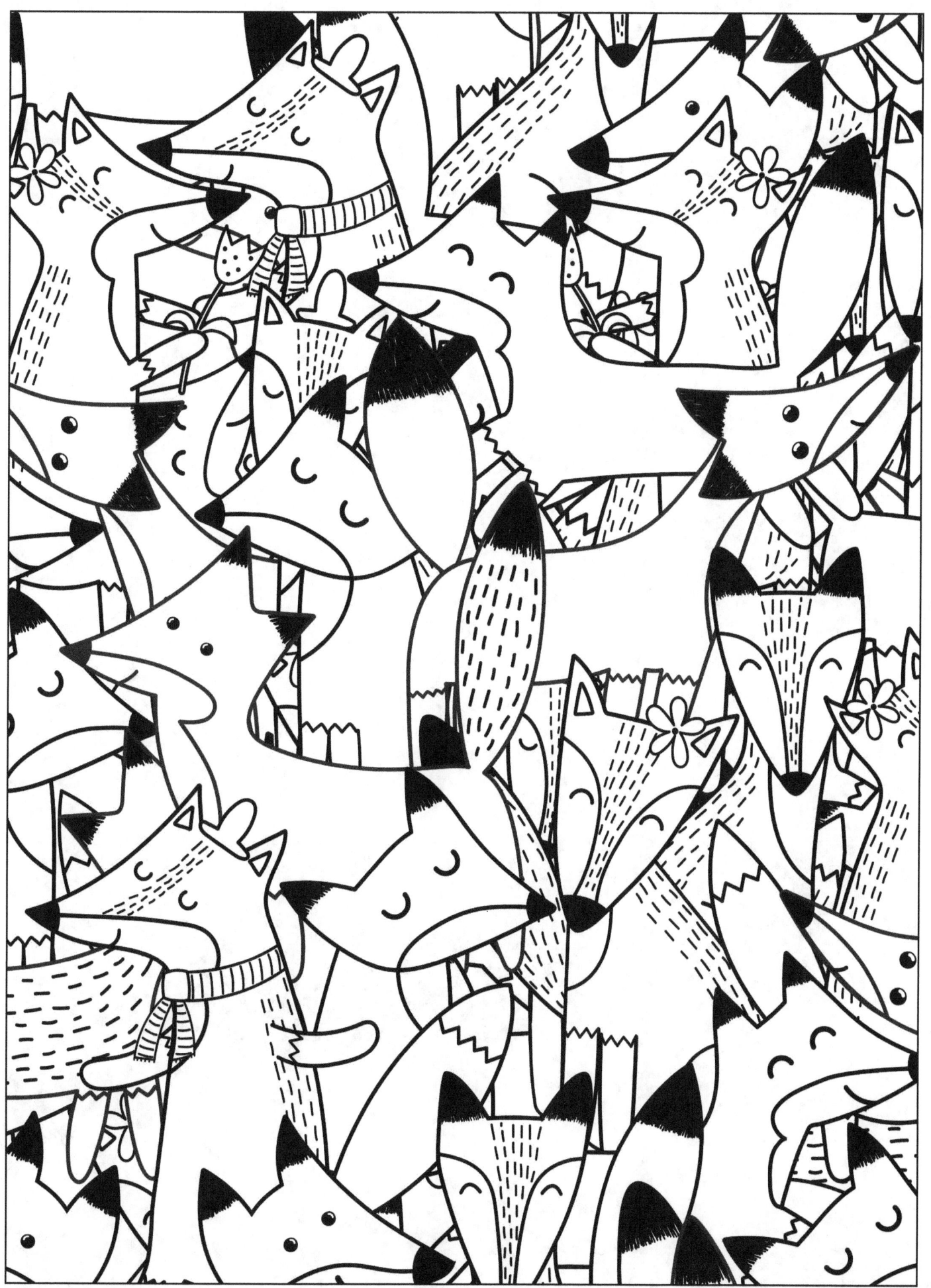

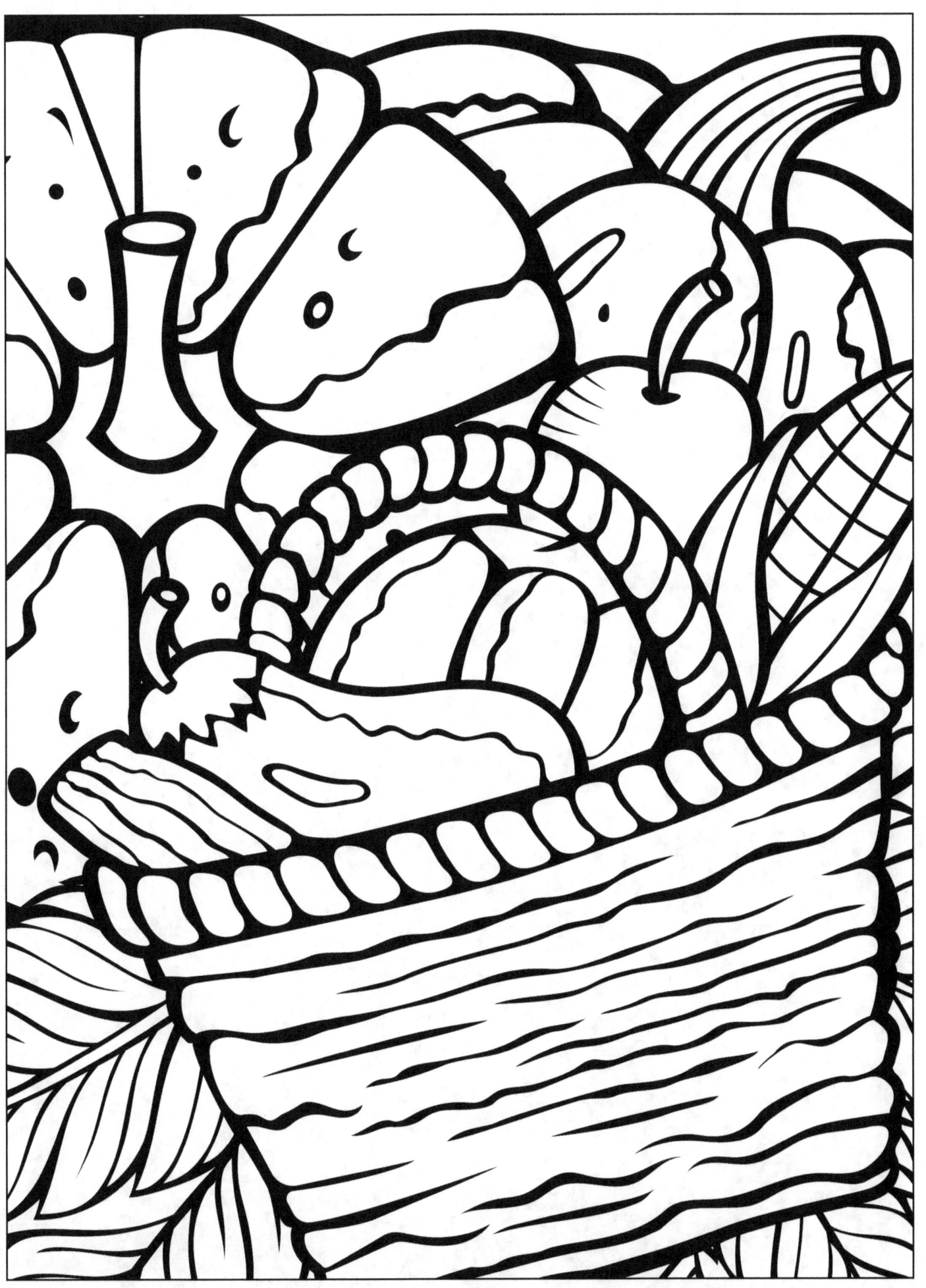

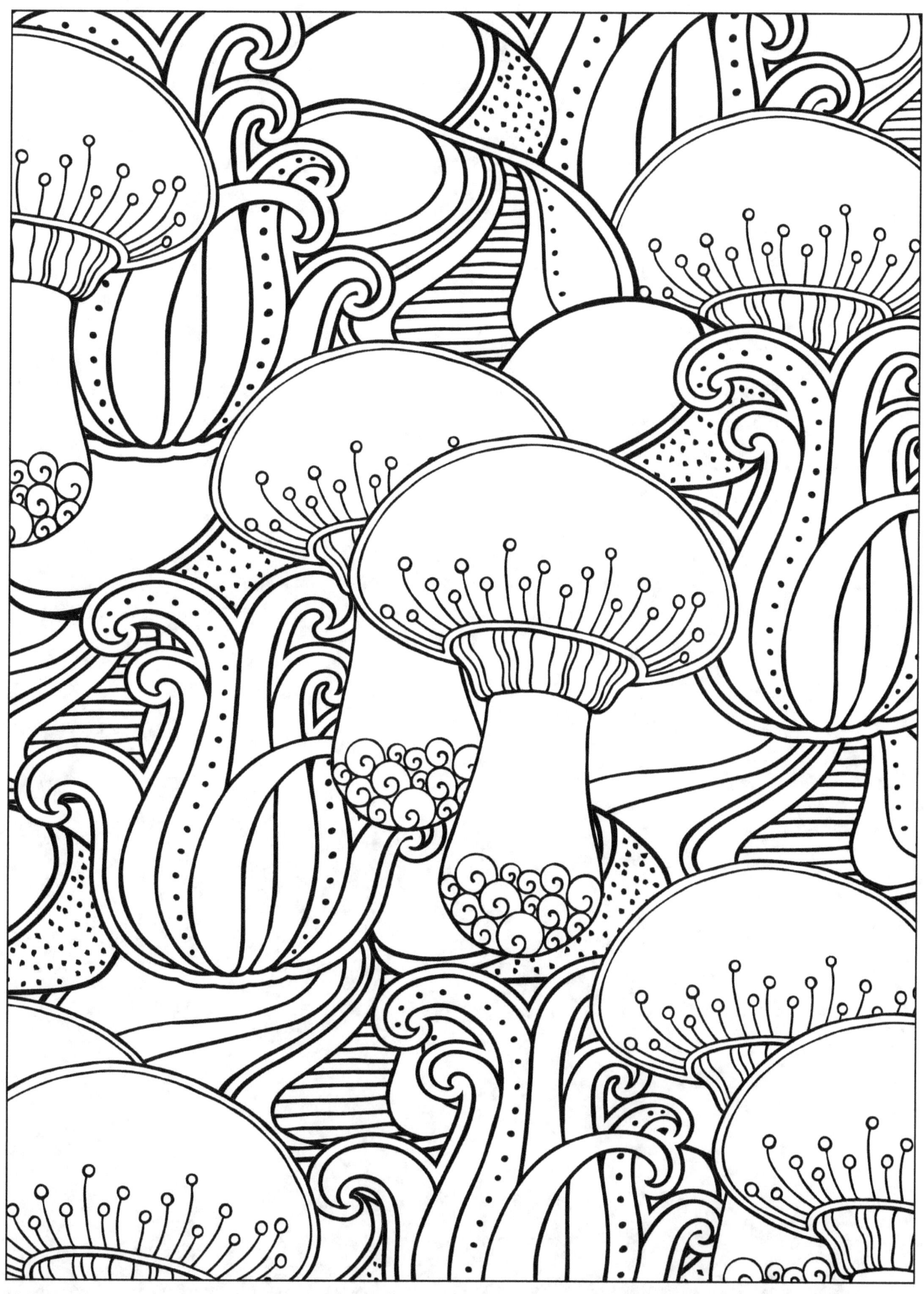

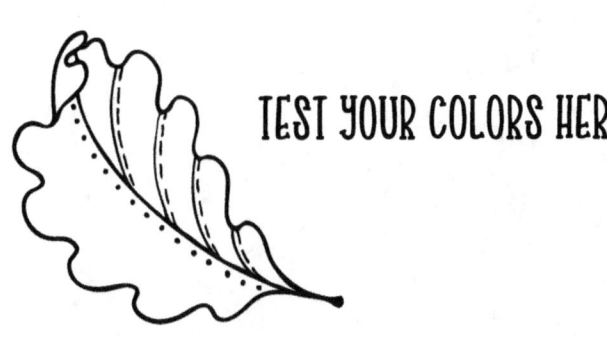

TEST YOUR COLORS HERE.

www.ingramcontent.com/pod-product-compliance
Lightning Source LLC
Chambersburg PA
CBHW081739220526
45468CB00008B/2164